D0828386

Can You Tell a Brachiosaurus from an Apatosaurus?

Buffy Silverman

Lerner Publications Company
Minneapolis

To Emma, one of my favorite plant eaters

Lerner Publications Company
A division of Lerner Publishing Group, Inc.
241 First Avenue North
Minneapolis, MN 55401 U.S.A.

Website address: www.lernerbooks.com

Library of Congress Cataloging-in-Publication Data

Silverman, Buffy.
    Can you tell a Brachiosaurus from an Apatosaurus? / by Buffy Silverman.
        p.   cm. — (Lightning Bolt Books™—Dinosaur Look-Alikes)
    Includes index.
    ISBN 978-1-4677-1360-3 (lib. bdg. : alk. paper)
    ISBN 978-1-4677-1755-7 (eBook)
    1. Brachiosaurus—Juvenile literature. 2. Apatosaurus—Juvenile literature. 3. Dinosaurs—Juvenile literature. I. Title.
    QE862.S3S483 2014
    567.913—dc23   2012046438

Manufactured in the United States of America
1 — PP — 7/15/13

Table of Contents

Legs: Front and Back

Dinosaurs lived on Earth millions of years before people. The largest dinosaurs belonged to a group called sauropods.

Sauropods towered over other dinosaurs.

Sauropods had long tails and long necks. Their heads looked tiny.

Sauropods walked on land.
They were huge and heavy.
They needed strong legs
to get around.

A sauropod's strong legs
supported its big body.

Brachiosaurus and Apatosaurus were both sauropods. They looked a lot alike. They both had long necks and long tails. But you can tell these dinosaurs apart.

Which sauropod is a Brachiosaurus, and which is an Apatosaurus?

Look at the front legs of this Brachiosaurus. These legs were longer than the back legs.

The upper bone of a Brachiosaurus front leg was 7 feet (2.2 meters) long. That's taller than most grown men!

Apatosaurus had
giant legs too. But
its front legs were
shorter than its
back legs.

Reaching for Plants

Brachiosaurus and Apatosaurus ate hundreds of pounds of plants each day.

Imagine eating as much as a sauropod. You'd need to munch hundreds of heads of lettuce a day!

Brachiosaurus and Apatosaurus needed a lot of energy to move their heavy bodies. They saved energy by staying in one place. They moved their long necks to find food.

Brachiosaurus could reach higher than Apatosaurus. It held its neck upward. It ate plants that grew up high.

Giraffes use their long necks and tall front legs to reach leaves. So did Brachiosaurus.

Brachiosaurus grabbed tree ferns and other tall plants. Its tall front legs helped it reach high places.

Scientists think Apatosaurus held its neck closer to the ground. It ate low-growing plants. It probably found ferns along rivers. It might have searched lakes for water plants.

Brachiosaurus had twelve
bones inside its long neck.
The bones were hollow
but strong.

Each neck bone was
about as long as a
child's baseball bat.

Apatosaurus had fifteen bones inside its neck. Its bones were hollow too. The bones were half as long as Brachiosaurus neck bones.

You have seven bones in your neck. The bones are much smaller than Apatosaurus neck bones!

Teeth Tales

Dinosaur teeth came in different shapes. The shape shows us what and how a dinosaur ate.

This is a tooth from Rebbachisaurus, another sauropod that ate plants.

Apatosaurus had long, peg-shaped teeth. Its teeth could strip soft leaves off plants.

Brachiosaurus could stuff its mouth full of plants.

Brachiosaurus teeth were shaped like spoons. Spoon-shaped teeth let it grab lots of tough leaves.

Neither dinosaur chewed its food. They swallowed leaves whole. They also swallowed stones. The stones helped grind up the leaves.

What happened when these big eaters could not find enough food? Scientists think they might have migrated. That means they both traveled in large groups called herds.

Herds of sauropods moved to find food.

Big and Bigger

Apatosaurus stood as high as a three-story building. It was longer than two school buses.

This Apatosaurus skeleton is 80 feet (24 m) long!

Brachiosaurus was even bigger. It reached the height of a four-story building. It was longer than three school buses.

Almost half of Apatosaurus' length was its tail. It could move its tail like a huge whip. The whipping tail might have boomed like a cannon!

Apatosaurus' tail was huge!

Brachiosaurus had a long tail too. But it was shorter than Apatosaurus' tail.

Adult Apatosaurus and Brachiosaurus were so big that predators did not attack them. But many of their eggs and young were eaten.

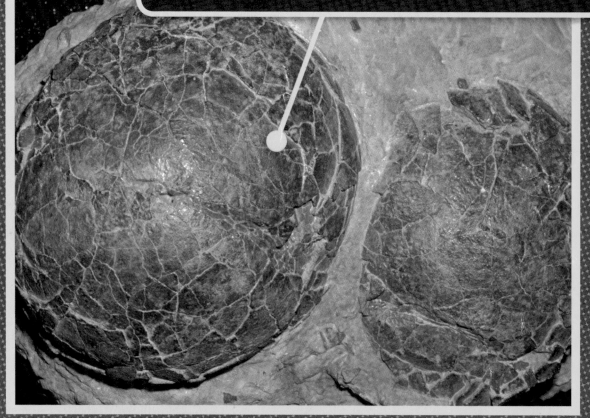

Predators are animals that hunt other animals. Predators hunted for Apatosaurus and Brachiosaurus eggs.

Young sauropods that survived grew quickly. Soon they grew big enough to stand up to hungry predators.

Dino Diagrams

Can you tell these dinosaurs apart?

Small head

Long neck

Thick, strong legs

Longer tail

Apatosaurus

Brachiosaurus

Small head

Long neck

Tall front legs

Strong back legs

Shorter tail

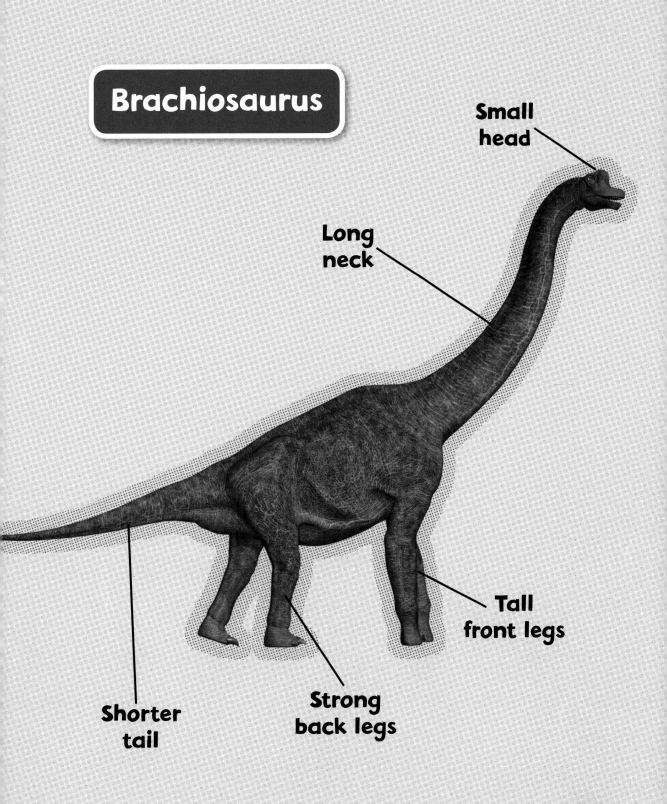

Glossary

energy: the ability to do work

herd: a group of animals of the same kind that
stay together

hollow: having an open space inside

migrate: to move from one place to another

predator: an animal that eats another animal

sauropod: a dinosaur that belonged to a group of
large plant eaters that had long necks, long tails,
and small heads

Further Reading

Brecke, Nicole, and Patricia M. Stockland. *Dinosaurs and Other Prehistoric Creatures You Can Draw.* Minneapolis: Millbrook Press, 2010.

Dinosaur Facts: Brachiosaurus Facts for Kids—Science Kids
http://www.sciencekids.co.nz/sciencefacts/dinosaurs/brachiosaurus.html

Dinosaurs—Natural History Museum
http://www.nhm.ac.uk/kids-only/dinosaurs/index.html

Hartland, Jessie. *How the Dinosaur Got to the Museum.* Maplewood, NJ: Blue Apple Books, 2011.

Lessem, Don. *National Geographic Kids Ultimate Dinopedia: The Most Complete Dinosaur Reference Ever.* Washington, DC: National Geographic, 2010.

Paleontology: The Big Dig—American Museum of Natural History
http://www.amnh.org/explore/ology/paleontology/?pop=29641#http://www.amnh.org/ology/features/livinglarge

Index

Photo Acknowledgments

The images in this book are used with the permission of: © Ralf Kraft/Dreamstime.com, pp. 1 (both) 24, 30 (left); © Dorling Kindersley/Getty Images, p. 2; © Roger Harris/ Science Source, p. 4; © francesco tomasinelli/TIPS/Photoshot, p. 5; © Louie Psihoyos/ Science Faction/SuperStock, pp. 6, 11, 16, 19; © Linda Bucklin/Dreamstime.com, pp. 7 (left), 29; © Andreas Meyer/Dreamstime.com, p. 7 (right); © Corey Ford/Bigstock.com, pp. 8, 27; © DEA Picture Library/De Agostini Picture Library/Getty Images, pp. 9, 20, 21; © Jim Zuckerman/CORBIS, p. 10; © Tobias Schwartz/CORBIS, p. 12; © Anup Shah/Taxi/ Getty Images, p. 13; © Kevin Schafer/Peter Arnold/Getty Images, p. 14; © Dorling Kindersly RF/Thinkstock, p. 15; © Colin Keates/Dorling Kindersley/Getty Images, p. 17; REUTERS/Tomas Bravo, p. 18; AP Photo/Skip Butler, p. 22; © Sefano Paterna/Alamy, p. 23; © Julius T. Csotonyi, http://csotonyi.com, p. 25; © Carlyn Iverson/Science Source, p. 26; © Encyclopaedia Britannica/UIG/Getty Images, p. 28; Andrew Kerr/ Dorling Kindersley/Getty Images.

Front cover: © Ralf Kraft/Dreamstime.com (top); © Linda Bucklin/Dreamstime.com (bottom).

Main body text set in Johann Light 30/36.